# MILITARY
# HELICOPTERS

BY DENNY VON FINN

150

160

TORQUE

BELLWETHER MEDIA • MINNEAPOLIS, MN

Are you ready to take it to the extreme?
Torque books thrust you into the action-packed world
of sports, vehicles, and adventure. These books may
include dirt, smoke, fire, and dangerous stunts.
**WARNING:** read at your own risk.

This edition first published in 2010 by Bellwether Media, Inc.

No part of this publication may be reproduced in whole or in part without written permission of the publisher.
For information regarding permission, write to Bellwether Media, Inc., Attention: Permissions Department,
5357 Penn Avenue South, Minneapolis, MN 55419.

Library of Congress Cataloging-in-Publication Data

Von Finn, Denny.
 Military helicopters / by Denny Von Finn.
    p. cm. -- (Torque books: the world's fastest)
 Summary: "Amazing photography accompanies engaging information about military helicopters. The
combination of high-interest subject matter and light text is intended for students in grades 3 through
7"--Provided by publisher.
 Includes bibliographical references and index.
 ISBN 978-1-60014-336-6 (hardcover : alk. paper)
 1. Military helicopters--Juvenile literature.  I. Title.
 UG1230.V66 2010
 623.74'6047--dc22                              2009037941

Text copyright © 2010 by Bellwether Media, Inc.
Printed in the United States of America, North Mankato, MN.

010110   1149

# CONTENTS

# What Are Military Helicopters?

Military helicopters are the world's fastest helicopters. They are designed for many different missions. Some military helicopters are used for search-and-rescue. Others are used to battle the enemy. Large military helicopters are used to transport troops. The safety of pilots and troops depends on the speed of these helicopters.

5

main rotors

Helicopters have **main rotors** on top of their body. These spinning blades let military helicopters move quickly. The main rotors also give pilots the ability of **vertical take-off and landing (VTOL)**.

World War II taught militaries the value of VTOL. **Fixed-wing** aircraft need a runway to take off and land. A helicopter needs only a small area called a **pad**. This makes helicopters important in small combat zones. Helicopters can take off and land from building roofs, jungle clearings, and Navy ships.

# Military Helicopter Technology

Main rotors give helicopters **lift** when they spin. The longest main rotors are 115 feet (35 meters) across. These are found on the Russian Mil V-12. This is the world's largest helicopter.

Mil V-12

tail rotor

A **tail rotor** is attached at the end of the **boom**. The spinning tail rotor works against the main rotor. This keeps the helicopter from spinning out of control. Rotor blades are often made of lightweight **composites**.

Today's fastest helicopters have **turboshaft** engines. Hot gases inside a turboshaft engine expand and spin **turbines**. These turbines are attached to the **shaft**. The shaft then causes the rotors to spin.

Turboshaft engines produce over 1,000 horsepower. That's more than six times the power of a normal car engine! Helicopters with turboshaft engines have top speeds of around 200 miles (322 kilometers) per hour.

## Fast Fact

The Russian Mil Mi-26 helicopter has two turboshaft engines. They each create more than 11,000 horsepower!

It takes great skill to fly a helicopter. The nose must be pointed downward to move the helicopter forward. The **cockpit** has foot pedals and a stick called the **cyclic control**. These controls work together to make the helicopter go up, down, or **hover**. They also make it move forward or backward.

Lynx ZB-500

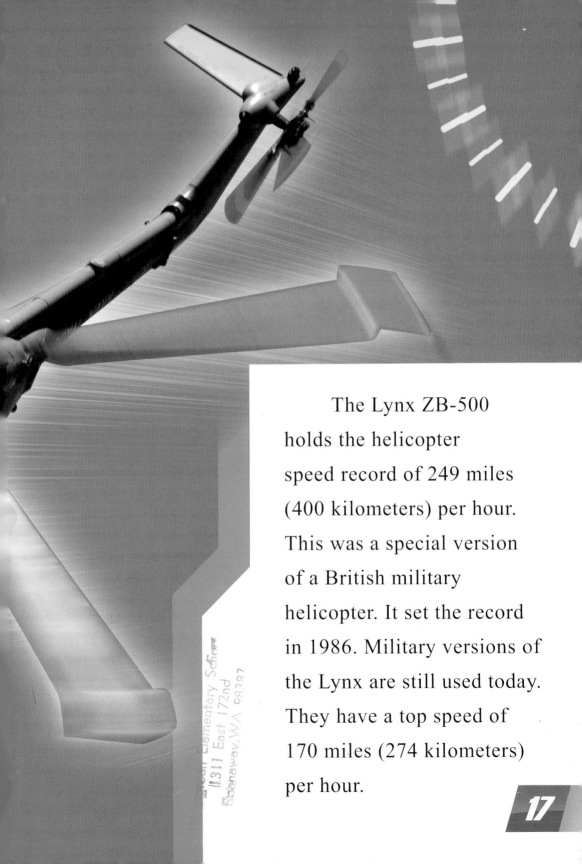

The Lynx ZB-500
holds the helicopter
speed record of 249 miles
(400 kilometers) per hour.
This was a special version
of a British military
helicopter. It set the record
in 1986. Military versions of
the Lynx are still used today.
They have a top speed of
170 miles (274 kilometers)
per hour.

# The Future of Military Helicopters

Today's fastest helicopters have top speeds of around 200 miles (322 kilometers) per hour. Sikorsky Aircraft plans to beat that record. Helicopters based on their X2 design could go 287 miles (464 kilometers) per hour. Militaries would use these helicopters to carry out missions very quickly.

X2

## Fast Fact

Helicopters with two main rotors like the X2 are easier to fly. The rotors work against each other. This removes the need for a tail rotor.

**Fire Scout**

Many people think the future of military helicopters is limited. A hovering helicopter is an easy target for enemies. The answer may be **drones**.

One drone being developed is the Fire Scout. It could hover 20,000 feet (6,100 meters) over the battlefield. The pilot could safely control this fast helicopter drone from thousands of miles away.

## Fast Fact

The Fire Scout could cruise at a speed of more than 125 miles (201 kilometers) per hour.

# GLOSSARY

**boom**—the long section of a helicopter that looks like a tail

**cockpit**—the area in a helicopter where the pilot sits

**composites**—hard manmade fabrics coated in plastic

**cyclic control**—the stick used by a pilot to help control a helicopter

**drones**—unmanned aircraft

**fixed-wing**—an aircraft with wings that don't move

**hover**—to stay in one place in the air

**lift**—a force that allows an aircraft to leave the ground

**main rotor**—the set of spinning blades on top of a helicopter

**pad**—a space where a helicopter takes off and lands

**shaft**—the long, stiff rod to which a helicopter's main rotors are attached

**tail rotor**—the spinning blade at the end of a helicopter's boom

**turbine**—a spinning, fan-like device found inside a turboshaft engine

**turboshaft**—a kind of engine that uses hot, expanding gases to spin a shaft

**vertical take-off and landing (VTOL)**—the ability to take off and land without a runway

# TO LEARN MORE

## AT THE LIBRARY

Alvarez, Carlos. *MH-53J Pave Lows*. Minneapolis, Minn.: Bellwether Media, 2010.

David, Jack. *Apache Helicopters*. Minneapolis, Minn.: Bellwether Media, 2008.

David, Jack. *HH-60 Pave Hawk Helicopters*. Minneapolis, Minn.: Bellwether Media, 2009.

## ON THE WEB

Learning more about military helicopters is as easy as 1, 2, 3.

1. Go to www.factsurfer.com.

2. Enter "military helicopters" into the search box.

3. Click the "Surf" button and you will see a list of related Web sites.

With factsurfer.com, finding more information is just a click away.

# INDEX

The images in this book are reproduced through the courtesy of: Craig McAteer,
front cover, pp. 16-17; EcoPrint, pp. 4-5; Hideo Kurihara / Alamy, p. 6; United
States Department of Defense, pp. 7, 14, 15, 20, 21; Stocktrek/ Getty Images, pp.
8-9; Bernhard Gröhl, p. 10; Jeffrey Zavitski, p. 11; Ivan Cholakov Gostock-dot-
net, pp. 12-13; Associated Press, pp. 18-19.